–FOODS OF–
THAILAND

by Christine Velure Roholt

BELLWETHER MEDIA • MINNEAPOLIS, MN

Library of Congress Cataloging-in-Publication Data

VeLure Roholt, Christine, author.
 Foods of Thailand / by Christine VeLure Roholt.
    pages cm. -- (Express. Cook with Me)
 Summary: "Information accompanies step-by-step instructions on how to cook Thai food. The text
level and subject matter are intended for students in grades 3 through 7"-- Provided by publisher.
 Audience: Age 7-12.
 Audience: Grades 3-7.
 Includes bibliographical references and index.
 ISBN 978-1-62617-122-0 (hardcover : alk. paper)
 1. Cooking, Thai--Juvenile literature. 2. Food habits--Thailand--Juvenile literature. 3. Thailand--Social
life and customs--Juvenile literature. I. Title.
 TX724.5.T5V45 2014
 641.59'593--dc23
                           2014008263

This edition first published in 2015 by Bellwether Media, Inc.

Printed in the United States of America, North Mankato, MN.

Table of Contents

Cooking the Thai Way

Thai **cuisine** is influenced by the food **traditions** of many cultures, especially Chinese, Indian, and Malaysian. Thai cooks fry, stir-fry, and deep-fry some foods like the Chinese. They modify Indian dishes with their own ingredients. Coconut oil replaces buttery *ghee*. Lemongrass and other herbs take the place of traditional Indian spices.

Thai cooks prepare spicy and mild dishes to be eaten together. They do this to create **harmony** at dinnertime. Fish sauce, or *nam pla*, is one ingredient that unites most Thai food. Many say it has a disgusting smell but makes food taste great.

nam pla

Hot, Hot, Hot

Missionaries from Portugal introduced Thai people to chilies. Red, green, or yellow chilies are included in many Thai dishes.

Eating the Thai Way

In Thailand, families sit down together to share main meals. Many Thai people believe eating meals alone brings bad luck. However, Thai people will often visit **street stalls** to pick up snacks between meals.

Feast on the Floor

Some people in Thailand's countryside sit on the ground to enjoy meals. This is the traditional way of eating a Thai meal.

No knife is needed when enjoying Thai food. Food is usually prepared in bite-sized amounts. The left hand holds a fork and the right hand holds a spoon. The fork is never brought to the mouth. Rather, it is used for pushing food onto the spoon. Thai people use their hands to eat the sticky rice that is served with most meals.

7

Regional Foods

Thai food is not the same in every part of the country. The North and South favor different amounts of spice in dishes. Each region also has its own version of rice, an important **staple**. Plain rice is served in the South and Central regions, and sticky rice is popular in the North.

North

nam prik ong:
Spicy chili dip with ground pork

Central

tom yum goong:
Spicy soup with fresh shrimp and lemongrass

Where is Thailand?

N
W E
S

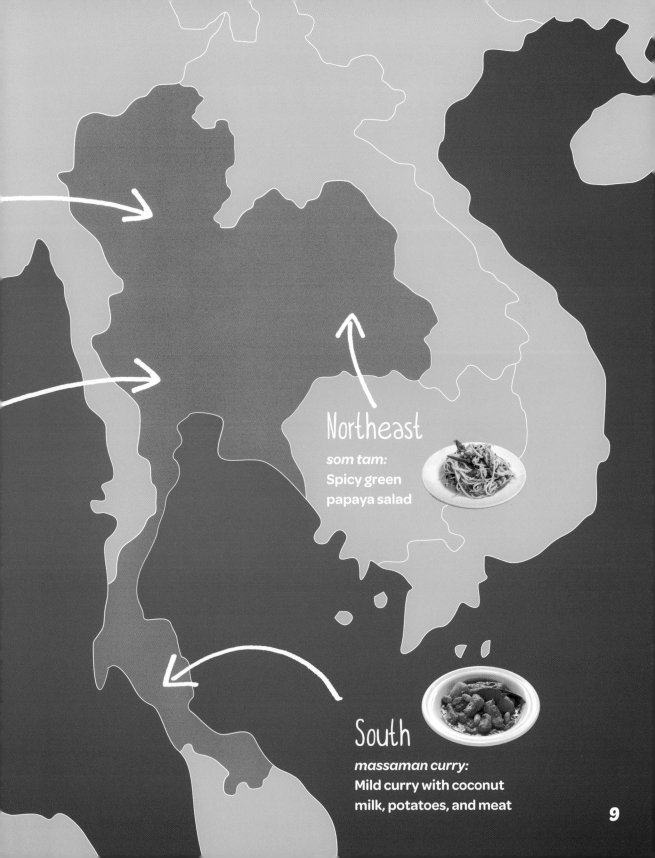

Northeast

som tam:
Spicy green
papaya salad

South

massaman curry:
Mild curry with coconut
milk, potatoes, and meat

Iced Drinks and Fruity Flavors

Thai people pair iced drinks with hot food and hot temperatures to cool off. Thai iced tea is a spiced black tea sweetened with sugar and **condensed milk**. Coffee can be used instead of tea to create Thai iced coffee.

Thai iced coffee

Thai iced tea

lychee

Beverage in a Bag

In Thailand, it is common to drink a beverage out of a plastic bag using a straw.

Fruits are the most common sweets in Thailand. People eat them as desserts. They also squeeze them to create a variety of **tropical** fruit juices. Flavors include guava, **lychee**, and passion fruit. Coconut water is also a popular beverage in Thailand. It is sweet and nutty, and it is often sipped straight from a coconut.

Getting Ready to Cook

Before you begin cooking, read these safety reminders. Make sure you also read the recipes you will follow. You will want to gather all the ingredients and cooking tools right away.

Safety Reminders

 Ask an adult for permission to start cooking. An adult should be near when you use kitchen appliances or a sharp knife.

 Wash your hands with soapy water before you start cooking. Wash your hands again if you lick your fingers or handle raw meat.

 If you have long hair, tie it back. Remove any bracelets or rings that you have on.

 Wear an apron when you cook. It will protect food from dirt and your clothes from spills and splatters.

 Always use oven mitts when handling hot cookware. If you accidentally burn yourself, run the burned area under cold water and tell an adult.

 If a fire starts, call an adult immediately. Never throw water on a fire. Baking soda can smother small flames. A lid can put out a fire in a pot or pan. If flames are large and leaping, call 911 and leave the house.

 Clean up the kitchen when you are done cooking. Make sure all appliances are turned off.

Khao Neeo Mamuang

COW NEE-oh ma-MWAHANG

Warm Treat

Even though it is often very hot in the summer, Thai people find this dessert most refreshing when served warm.

Sweet Sticky Rice

Serves 4

Khao neeo mamuang is a popular summer dessert sold by street carts, restaurants, and markets throughout Thailand. This sticky rice dish is sweetened with coconut milk and is often served with fresh mangos, which are commonly grown in Thailand.

What You'll Need

- 2 cups Thai long grain sticky rice (substitute: sweet rice)
- 3 1/2 cups water
- 1/2 teaspoon salt
- 3 sliced mangos
- large pot with cover
- saucepan

Let's Make It!

1

Add the rice and water to a large pot, then let the rice soak for 1-4 hours.

2

Stir in the salt, then bring to a boil over high heat.

3

Reduce to medium-low heat, then cover. Leave a slight crack for steam to escape, then cook for about 10 minutes.

4

When the rice is cooked, remove from heat. Stir in the sauce, then cover and let cool.

5

Transfer the rice to bowls, then serve with the chopped mangos.

Enjoy!

Make the Sauce

Many people serve *khao neeo mamuang* with a sweet sauce. Make your own sauce with the following ingredients:

- 1 1/2 cups coconut milk
- 1/2 teaspoon salt
- 1/2 cup sugar

To prepare the sauce, mix all ingredients, bring to a boil, and then remove from heat.

Gai Yang

gai YONG

Thai Grilled Chicken
Serves 4

Gai yang is a favorite street food found throughout Thailand. Each region offers a variety of ingredients. However, each recipe calls for marinating the chicken for several hours before grilling.

What You'll Need

- 3 pounds chicken breast, legs, and wings
- 1 stalk lemongrass
- 3 garlic cloves
- 2 teaspoons black pepper
- 3 tablespoons fish sauce
- 1 cup unsweetened coconut milk
- mortar and pestle

- large bowl
- spatula
- tongs
- plastic wrap
- broiler pan

Let's Make It!

1

Using a mortar and pestle, make a paste out of the lemongrass, garlic, and black pepper.

2

Transfer the paste to a large bowl. Add the fish sauce and coconut milk, then mix well.

3

Add the chicken to the bowl. Make sure to coat each piece well.

4

Cover the bowl with plastic wrap, then refrigerate for at least 1 hour.

5

Set the chicken on a lightly oiled broiler pan. Set an oven rack about 6 inches from the broiler, then turn on the broiler.

6

Broil the chicken for about 10 minutes, then brush the chicken with more marinade. Flip the pieces, then broil for another 10 minutes.

Side of Rice

Gai yang is often served with a side of sticky rice.

Jok

joke

Breakfast to Go

Street vendors often sell jok in plastic bags. It is then transferred to a bowl before being eaten.

Thai Rice Porridge
Serves 4

Jok is a popular breakfast comfort food sold by street stalls and in marketplaces throughout Thailand. This thick porridge gets its rich flavor from the meat and herbs added.

What You'll Need

- 2 1/2 cups jasmine rice
- 8-10 cups water
- 1 tablespoon olive oil
- 1 pound ground pork (substitute: chicken or beef)
- 4-6 chopped garlic cloves
- 2 inches ginger root, peeled and chopped
- 2 tablespoons fish sauce
- 2 tablespoons soy sauce
- sliced green onion
- grated ginger
- grated garlic
- fresh cilantro leaves
- black pepper
- colander
- large bowl
- large pot
- large frying pan
- spatula

Let's Make It!

1

Add the uncooked rice to a colander and rinse with water for about 2 minutes.

2

Transfer the rice to a large pot. Add 5 cups of water, then cook over medium heat for about 30 minutes.

3

Pour the olive oil in a large pan over medium heat. Add the meat, garlic, chopped ginger, 1 tablespoon of the fish sauce, and 1 tablespoon of the soy sauce. Sauté for 10–15 minutes.

4

When the rice has cooked for 30 minutes, add the meat mixture to the large pot. Stir in 2 cups of water and the remaining soy and fish sauces. Reduce heat to a simmer.

5

Cook for about 60 minutes, stirring well and adding water as needed. The mixture's consistency should be thick and creamy. Add soy sauce and fish sauce to taste.

6

Scoop the rice into bowls. Serve with sliced green onion, grated ginger, garlic, cilantro, and pepper.

Enjoy!

19

Pad Thai

pahd TIE

Stir-fried Noodles
Serves 4

Pad Thai is a famous stir-fried noodle dish most commonly served in Thailand by street carts. Though many people believe that it was first prepared in China, it was made popular by Thailand's Prime Minister in the 1930s and 1940s.

What You'll Need

- 8 ounces dried wide rice noodles
- 1 tablespoon tamarind paste
- 2 tablespoons fish sauce
- 1 tablespoon brown sugar
- 1 tablespoon lime juice
- 2 tablespoons water
- 2 tablespoons olive oil
- 2 minced garlic cloves
- 1 inch peeled and minced ginger root
- 4 cups broccoli florets
- 2 sliced carrots
- 3 sliced scallions
- 1 cup bean sprouts
- 2 eggs
- large bowl
- mixing bowl
- large frying pan
- whisk
- tongs

Let's Make It!

1

Add the noodles to a bowl of cold water. Let sit for 60 minutes or until noodles are soft. Drain the water.

2

To make the sauce, combine the tamarind paste, fish sauce, brown sugar, lime juice, and 2 tablespoons of water in a bowl, then mix well.

3

Pour 1 tablespoon of olive oil in a large pan over high heat, then add the garlic and ginger. Cook for 30 seconds. Add the broccoli and carrots, then cook for about 3 minutes.

4

Transfer the vegetables to a bowl, then mix in the scallions and bean sprouts.

5

Pour 1 tablespoon of olive oil in the pan over medium heat, then add the eggs. Use a whisk to scramble.

6

Add the noodles to the eggs, then cook for 1 minute.

Enjoy!

Stir in the sauce and vegetables to the pan, then cook for about 3 minutes or until the noodles are ready. Top with chopped peanuts.

Bangkok and Beyond

In the 1940s, the Thai government released a recipe for pad Thai to create a national food for its people. The dish's popularity quickly spread from Bangkok to small villages, eventually becoming popular around the world.

21

Glossary

condensed milk—canned milk that is thick and sweet

cuisine—a style of cooking unique to a certain area or group of people

harmony—peace or balance

lychee—a small, sweet fruit with a hard outer skin

staple—a food that is widely and regularly eaten

street stalls—places where people sell food or other things in the street

traditions—customs, ideas, or beliefs that have been passed down from one generation to the next

tropical—part of the tropics; the tropics is a hot, rainy region near the equator.

To Learn More

AT THE LIBRARY

Kummer, Patricia K. *The Food of Thailand*. New York, N.Y.: Marshall Cavendish Benchmark, 2012.

Locricchio, Matthew. *The Cooking of Thailand*. New York, N.Y.: Marshall Cavendish Benchmark, 2012.

Simmons, Walter. *Thailand*. Minneapolis, Minn.: Bellwether Media, 2011.

ON THE WEB

Learning more about Thailand is as easy as 1, 2, 3.

1. Go to www.factsurfer.com.

2. Enter "Thailand" into the search box.

3. Click the "Surf" button and you will see a list of related web sites.

With factsurfer.com, finding more information is just a click away.

Index